NEPALI
CHILDREN'S BOOK
Learn Counting in Nepali by Coloring

SIMONE SEAMS

ILLUSTRATED BY DUY TRUONG

CONTENTS

ONE
एक

TWO
दुई

THREE
तिन

FOUR
चार

FIVE
पाँच

SIX

छ

SEVEN
सात

EIGHT
आठ

NINE
नौ

TEN
दस

ELEVEN
एघार

21

TWELVE

बाह

THIRTEEN
तेरह

FOURTEEN
चौध

FIFTEEN

पन्ध्र

Made in United States
Orlando, FL
23 November 2024

54361103R00020